Marian Wright Edelman
A Voice for Children

Karen Davila

Boston, Massachusetts
Chandler, Arizona
Glenview, Illinois
Upper Saddle River, New Jersey

Illustrations
Opener, 1, 2, 3, 4, 5, 6, 7 Christine Kornacki.

Copyright © 2013 by Pearson Education, Inc., or its affiliates. All rights reserved. Printed in the United States of America. This publication is protected by copyright, and permission should be obtained from the publisher prior to any prohibited reproduction, storage in a retrieval system, or transmission in any form by any means, electronic, mechanical, photocopying, recording, or likewise. For information regarding permissions, write to Pearson Curriculum Rights & Permissions, One Lake Street, Upper Saddle River, New Jersey 07458.

Pearson® is a trademark, in the U.S. and/or in other countries, of Pearson Inc. or its affiliates.

ISBN-13: 978-0-328-67571-5
ISBN-10:   0-328-67571-7

12 13 14 15 V0SI 18 17 16 15

Marian Wright Edelman does important work. She is a leader who helps children. She speaks with children, families, and **communities**. She tells others about their lives. Why did she choose to do this work?

When Edelman was a girl, her family worked to help their community. Later as a young woman, she joined a group that worked with families who were poor. She wanted to help them solve their problems.

Edelman felt that she could help solve community problems by doing more for children. In 1973, she started a **fund** to help children learn and stay healthy. She got others to offer their time, money, and skills.

Her fund gives children **health care**. It helps them have healthy food and safe places to live. It helps their families, too.

Her fund provides **education** that can help children solve problems. They learn to be kind, caring, and fair. They learn to be leaders in their communities. Children learn skills that help them get good jobs when they grow up.

Because of Edelman's work, children have grown up and helped their communities. Her fund keeps on helping children, families, and communities. You can see why people have called her "a voice for children."

Glossary

communities places where many people live and work together

education learning and teaching

fund money used for a special goal

health care medical help that keeps people well or helps them get better